T0161061

DAYS WHEN I HIDE MY CORPSE IN A CARDBOARD BOX

自我紙盒藏屍的日子

Selected Poetry of

Lok Fung

洛楓

Translated from the Chinese by Eleanor Goodman

Zephyr Press | **mccm**creations

Published in 2018 by

Zephyr Press   www.zephyrpress.org
MCCM Creations   www.mccmcreations.com

Book design by *type*slowly
Printed in Hong Kong

This title is part of the Hong Kong Atlas, a series of contemporary Hong Kong writing
in English translation. Funded primarily by the HKADC's Literature Translation Project,
and coordinated by the Faculty of Arts at Baptist University, these works include a broad
range of poetry, prose and graphic adaptations from established and emerging
Hong Kong authors.

The publishers acknowledge with gratitude the financial and administrative support
of the Hong Kong Arts Development Council, the Massachussets Cultural Council
and the Faculty of Arts at Baptist University.

The Hong Kong Arts Development Council fully supports freedom of artistic expression.
The views and opinions expressed in this project do not represent the stand of the Council.

Supported by

Cataloguing-in publication data is available from the Library of Congress.

ISBN 978-1-938890-18-5 (US)
978-988-77238-7-5 (HK)

CONTENTS

Translator's Foreword

Eleanor Goodman

Natalia Chan (Lok Fung) occupies a particularly multivalent space in the contemporary Sinophone literary world. Born and raised in the constantly shifting cultural, linguistic, and artistic landscape of Hong Kong, she has also traveled widely and holds a Ph.D. in comparative literature and cultural studies from UC San Diego. Despite this experience abroad, her poetry remains rooted in her native soil and native tongue of Hong Kong Cantonese.

Hong Kong's numerous contradictions make it a fertile, if increasingly uneasy, ground for myriad artists. The British influence remains evident on every street corner: in the English-language street names, the left-hand flow of traffic, the orderly queues and Western luxury brands. Yet, just as predominant are the layers of Cantopop, conversations in Cantonese, Chinese styles of architecture, the scent of joss sticks, durian and pungent clouds of tofu—all cast against what is often a stunning backdrop of lush green hills and sparkling metallic sky rises.

In these poems, however, Chan's Hong Kong is found less in the daily details and more in the intersections of pop culture, high art, politics, human relations and literary and feminist theory. Her roles as social critic, theorist and radio show host can be seen in her verse, which frequently approaches life, love and other universal questions from a distanced, if not ironic, angle. The internet, cellphones, TV shows and pop stars all figure significantly in her work, lending her writing a contemporary feel while simultaneously emphasizing the interconnectedness of this current moment, particularly in a global financial center such as Hong Kong.

Equally contemporary are her explorations of male/female relations and the role that procedures and artificial enhancements play in our conceptions of others and ourselves. In her poem "On Skin-Whitening Days," she writes:

On skin-whitening days
I politely refuse to go out
because I'm afraid of the light
and can't handle my friends' glittering lenses
their sympathy and understanding
seems scorching
when what actually kills is in the midst of multiplying cells

Because of love I've recently
developed allergic dark spots
it's a kind of passion
that ages over time
and embeds deep in the skin
a bit of sand polished by seafloor flora
can't rub away
a lifetime of lines

Expensive, painful and sometimes humiliating "beautifying" practices such as skin-whitening and hair-straightening are feminist issues that are also intertwined with personal relationships—both romantic and platonic, and perhaps most significantly, the relationship between the self and the imagined ideal self. These ideals bear an internal component, though they are largely created by social pressure and expectation; examples of unreasonable models for either gender remain seemingly ubiquitous in our modern media and cityscapes. Chan questions the place of these oppressive norms—while continuing to participate in them both consciously and ambivalently—which allows her to analyze and criticize from a powerful position: that of a true insider.

The same is true for the political poems in this volume, which include translations of work selected from several of Chan's award-winning collections. She carefully negotiates the delicate territory of Hong Kong independence and interdependence. At times Chan explicitly addresses the 1997 handover in poems such as "When the City Gets Old" and "October in the City: A Book of Amnesia," but the question of politics arises throughout this volume, as it does in daily life. Any mention of a passport, a language, a border, a barrier, money, the media are all inherently political. This is a politics of the small, that which affects our lives often in more immediately tangible ways than global networks and ambitions. Chan is able to build a remarkable scaffolding of the personal, even as her poems simultaneously operate on other political and theoretical levels.

As much as she lives the life of the mind, Natalia Chan is also deeply physical and tactile in her poetry. Her stanzas on dance—another of her artistic obsessions—employ movement and sensuality as a way to explore human relationships and emotions.

Dance, as a non-verbal art form, can work as a kind of counterbalance to poetry, which is arguably the most intensely verbal art form. Yet there are also overlaps between the two: gesture, tone, storytelling, musicality, illusion, allusion, empty and filled space. She navigates the distance and difference between dancer and audience, performer and choreographer with the confidence and agility of one who has herself played each of these roles. In "Interface" she writes:

I.

You dance your circumscribed space
I write my chiseled time
that was the way we happened to meet
fragments in splintered arcs
between 0 and 1
surroundings of scattered probability

II.

Left hand on right, you dance into the middle
right foot crossing over left, I hold my reputation between them
when the notes tremble like timid commas or a dotted line
I know that the heartbeat is a circle
and there is no way out

III.

You stretch out your fingers to draw the line of sight closer
when the rhythm of the music locks my movements
you come even closer

This interface is both virtual and tangible, and our contemporary dances frequently involve electronic pirouettes. Intimacy can now imply not only physical proximity, but also technological interconnectedness. Though these relationships seem to function primarily via text messages and video chats, the embodiedness of experience continues. Given that contemporary background, the very physicality and immediacy of dance takes on a multilayered significance: both old-fashioned and universal, compromised and uncompromising. For all of our virtual reality, physical contact, gesture and touch remain profoundly vital modes of communication. Chan emphasizes this in her intimate descriptions of dance and the experience of watching dance performances: both offer spaces in which "you lose the imprisonment of desire and let your limbs open and close."

Underpinning this experience is yet another sensory layer, namely the aurality of music. In the poem, this music might be an accompaniment to a partnered physical dance; it might also be a private experience, music played on a laptop to accompany a virtual chat from a distance, a dance of electrons. Chan plays off her references to music and rhythm in her verse, producing a rich musicality that I've done my best to capture in phrases such as "surroundings of scattered probability."

In her richly multifaceted work, Chan demonstrates that poetry—like music, like dance, like our human emotional experiences—remains far from irrelevant within the global financial maelstrom of Hong Kong. Her poems are imbued with the power to reflect and influence this current moment, and future moments to come, drawing popular culture, academic theory, politics and technology within the compass of her artistic expression.

DAYS WHEN I HIDE MY CORPSE
IN A CARDBOARD BOX

自我紙盒藏屍的日子

怨靈

凝望蝴蝶
便想起你從高處墮下的姿勢
可能中途會展翼高飛
因為碎裂
並不適合你的容顏
如同思念
只能如絲的帶走
不能凝固或消滅
但我知道
蝴蝶能飛卻飛得不遠
只能縈繞和徘徊
直至找到自己的怨靈

如果蝴蝶被標本
那是用軀體釘住死亡的斑彩
如果蝴蝶被雕塑
那是再生的力量將軀體變形和留存
但我知道
沒有一個夢能藏得住你
到時候我的妄念
只會被翻成一葉空白
遍體晶瑩
如同你給這人世間
當初婆娑、然後靈動
最後反擊的
靜止──

Angry Ghost

Staring at a butterfly
I think of the way you fell from on high
and maybe halfway down you unfolded
your wings and flew
because being shattered
didn't suit you
and like memory
it could only be taken away in threads
it couldn't solidify or perish
still I know
a butterfly can fly but never that far
it can only hover and circle
until it finds its own angry ghost

If a butterfly is kept as a specimen
death's colorful stripes are pinned down by the carcass
if a butterfly is painted
the body is preserved and transformed by the power of rebirth
but I know
no dream can keep you
when the time comes my illusions
will only translate into an empty space
the whole body glimmers
like what you gave this world
at first with your whirling dance, then your wit
and finally with a counterattack
of stillness   —

白髮中女傳

一梳梳到尾
再梳梳到白髮滿地
原本已經蒼老
是太陽黑子折射你異色的錯認
將我照成紅顏璀璨
空悲切

白髮而不能白首
霧起時城市有一種濕重
煙住你的視線
污染的空氣漲滿不能爆破的小水泡
浮浮降降在風中打成圈圈的欲說還休
寄身於無法辨別色溫的噪音裏
彼此不能避免被閒言撞擊
於是你有你細說從頭
我有我蓋棺定論
黑白之間是灰
生死的兩頭纏著風燭
晨光與蠟影祇能成灰不能承諾
從前和以後
一夜間無法回頭

放手吧　即使你有汗濕的驚恐
沒法承載空無一人的風景
但握著的不過輕如泡沫
總有一天魂飛魄散

Tale of a White-Haired Spinster

Combing down to the ends
combing again until white hair coats the floor
I'm already old
it's sunspots reflecting your colorful misidentification
that shine me into a young beauty
in mourning

White hair but not a whole white head
when the fog lifts the city is damp and heavy
misting over your vision
the smog swells up in unbreakable little bubbles
the undulating wind entwines with circles of stifled speech
that live in a din of undifferentiated color and warmth
and can't help but crash into gossip
so you have your old stories
and I have my foregone conclusions
between black and white is gray
life and death tangle into old age
daybreak and candles turn to dust and can't promise anything
in the past and future
any given night will never return

Let it go   even if you're sweat-soaked with terror
and you can't bear the deserted landscape
though what you hold is lighter than foam
there will be a day when you're senseless with fear

錄鬼簿上我比你提早到達孟婆橋
喝下了忘川便記不起你仍在流連忘返
誰叫我們的鐘擺有不能修正的時差
當紅顏不再白髮
便是你蒼老的時間

in the Book of Ghosts I reach the Wind Goddess Bridge before you
drinking of the River Lethe I forget you haven't come home
the clock tells us the time can't be set right
when beautiful women no longer grow white hair
that's when you'll be old

即溶愛情咖啡

最近愛上即溶咖啡
溶掉你　像溶掉我心
留下污漬
在牆壁、衣角和抽屜
發霉　沒有發臭
許是咖啡因已經過期
連閨怨也無法保鮮

是因為神探伽俐略才愛上咖啡
心跳、手震
與愛情的凶案無關
（誰是無辜的殺害者？）
跌宕、懸疑
和你的行蹤脫線
（你的不在場證明！）
偶爾會在網上發現
跟你同名同姓的人
但網海恢恢　疏而缺漏
我的死前留言如被肢解的屍身
總載浮載沉
祇好離座離線走長長的階梯
從前半生走到下半世

最後落腳空曠的天井抱著貓看天
清晨的陽光濕著昨夜的雨
鳥聲啞著城市的煙塵
貓的尾巴很短　比我的愛念長
倏忽鬆手便從此滑落
貓毛與虛無

8

Instant Love and Coffee

Recently I've fallen in love with instant coffee
dissolving you   like dissolving my heart
leaving dark stains
on the walls, clothing, drawers
mildewing   odorless
perhaps the caffeine has expired
not even love poetry can keep things fresh

I fell in love with coffee because of Detective Galileo
my heart leaps and hands tremble
but that has nothing to do with love's homicide case
(who murdered the innocent?)
boldness, suspense
and your whereabouts offline
(your alibi!)
once in a while on the web I'll discover
someone else with your name
but the internet is vast   scattered and uneven
my last note before I die will be like a dismembered corpse
bobbing up and down
it's better to go offline and climb a long flight of stairs
from the first half of your life to the second

At last I'm on the open patio with the cat watching the sky
the early morning sunlight is wet from last night's rain
the birdsong is hoarse from the city's pollution
the cat's tail is quite short   it's longer than my affection
I let go swiftly and off slips
cat fur and nothingness

我低頭對自己的影子發笑
舉頭尋找一片青天
祇得來一張藍幕的暈眩
像電腦的閃光
然後樓下傳來兇狠的狗吠
尖銳的嘶叫咬住我的聽覺不放
狼心　如鐵
我追著黑貓咒罵
胃裏一陣翻騰
決定再來一杯咖啡
溶掉你　像溶掉我心

I bow to my own shadow and smile
I lift my head to look for a bit of clear sky
but all I see is a dizzying blue curtain
like the flickering of a computer screen
then a ferocious barking drifts up from a lower floor
the sharp yapping sinks its teeth into my senses
a wolf heart   like iron
I chase the black cat cursing
my stomach churns
I decide to have another cup of coffee
dissolving you   like dissolving my heart

鬼節恩仇錄

扮成骷髏、蜘蛛或神奇女俠
穿上才子、佳人、巫婆或魔術師的裝束
從七夕鬼節到十月的Halloween
我們總算看清彼此的面目了
如今新舊鬼節都已成過去
新仇舊恨也燒成了節日的死灰
無須假裝拍案驚奇
或爾虞我詐了
我們都是熟練的演藝者
懂得甚麼時候落妝、下台
然後謝幕

縱使這並不是一個很圓滿的結局
例如骷髏甩了手
蜘蛛斷了爪
才子錯配巫婆
女俠的魔術又平平無奇
但事已至此
就讓發生的繼續發生吧

為了跟你演這齣傳奇
才學會化妝的技法
塗上粉底、眼影和唇彩
原來可以讓五官這樣接近真實
也許你會覺得有點陌生
不打緊
反正與你無關了

Gratitude and Enmity at the Ghost Festival

Dressed up as a skeleton, a spider, or Wonder Woman
wearing the clothes of scholars, beauties, witches, and magicians
between Ghost Festival in July and Halloween in October
we can finally see each other's faces
these days the Ghost Festival is part of the past
bundles of resentment are burnt to holiday embers
there's no need to feign surprise
or deceive one another
we're both practiced performers
and know when to stop the act and leave the stage
and when to come back for the curtain call

Even if there is no happy ending
if a skeleton loses a hand
or a spider breaks a leg
a scholar is mismatched with a witch
Wonder Woman's magic is mediocre and dull
when it gets that bad
let's just let things take their course

To perform these dramas with you
this scholar learned how to wear makeup
applying foundation, eye shadow and lipstick
to make the features look more real
it might seem unfamiliar to you
but it doesn't matter
it has nothing to do with you anyway

我的妝容只留給鏡子
不為甚麼
只為它忠誠的反照
即使欺瞞
也信守一生一世

明天或明年
仍有新的節慶循環
但無論披上怎樣的裝扮
我都不打算和你互相確認了
因為蠟炬成灰
並不是吉祥的遊戲
何況燒蠟既危險又不環保
我們還是各自擱淺天涯和海角
坐看同一輪變臉的月
背向不同的心思
從此各有歸屬的潮汐

聖誕來時
我會扮成小鹿坐上雪車
離開你的視線
趕赴另一場沒有時限的
化妝舞會

my makeup is just for the mirror
and not for anything else
it's only for that loyal reflection
even if it lies to me
it will stand by me for a lifetime

Tomorrow or the next year
will bring a new cycle of festivals
but no matter what costume I throw on
I won't expect us to recognize each other
because a candle turning to ash
isn't a happy comedy
plus candle-burning is dangerous and bad for the environment
we're still stranded on our own separate promontories
sitting there looking at the same moon
we turn our backs on different thoughts
and so we belong to different tides

When Christmas comes
I'll play the fawn and sit in the sleigh
out of sight
rushing to another unending
masquerade

凝鏡．Flash Back

情勢急轉直下
你背著她看著我
我看著你背著她
祇有手提電話嗚嗚長鳴的訊息
無法解讀也拒絕聆聽
祇有百合花刺鼻的粉末在時間延宕的
空隙裏散播猜疑
扶手的欄杆開始失去支撐的身體
偏執的平台繼續無法進展的表情
於是——凝鏡——
然後——flash back——

早在離開洗手間的時候我遇見她
扭壞了水龍頭踏錯了梯級後我決定
從此抹走你的視線
返回劇院後我瞥見自己的座位
從未如此溫婉、寂靜和良善
於是立定主意用靈魂勾住你的身影
不管月光或死光從哪兒輻射
盲點或光點的暈盪間拍一張照片
當然你我沒有理由相信定鏡
能夠保住年月、微笑和親近
在快門按下的剎那你的髮膚
我的容顏早已死了
於是——flash back——
然後——凝鏡——

Freeze Frame   Flash Back

Then things took a sudden turn
you looked at me behind her back
behind her back I looked at you
there was only the whoosh of texts
indecipherable but impossible to ignore
in the time delay an acrid pollen of lilies
spread suspicion
the railing began to sag behind me
the slanted platform couldn't keep up its expression
and so——freeze frame——
then——flash back——

I met her leaving the bathroom
after breaking the tap and stumbling on the stairs I decided
I would avoid your gaze
I came back into the theater and glimpsed my seat
never so gentle, calm, and kind
I made up my mind to capture your image with my soul
regardless of radiating moonbeams or death rays
between blindspots and pixelated haloes I snapped a photo
of course you and I have no reason to believe a lens
can capture the moment, the smile, the intimacy
at the instant the shutter clicked, your body
and my looks had already died
and so——flash back——
then——freeze frame——

情勢依舊急轉直下
她向你移前你向我走近
欄杆扶著無法後退的腰我冷凍如
大理石像觸手冰涼彷彿沒有體溫
聽風的崖邊你我隨時掉落粉身碎骨
有人走過甬道但搞動不起僵化的氣流
木門被關上玻璃的掩映再開開合合
碎裂的倒照裏你驟然向我刺來
比仙人掌還要刻骨銘心的眼神
腳底便磨出沙礫的呼喚於是跟著你走
走過圍板、地氈、桌椅和空曠與虛無
走出被圈定的框框
甩掉死不悔改的凝鏡──再沒有flash back

Then things took another sudden turn
she found you before you could come to me
the railing pressed against my back and I was as frozen
as a marble statue with icy cold-blooded tentacles
we could have fallen to a bloody death from that windy cliff
someone passed by but didn't stir the fossilized air
the glass door was opened and shut by the shadows
and in the broken reflection you suddenly pierced me
your eyes sharper than cactus thorns
the crunch of gravel under foot followed you
past the borders, the carpet, tables and chairs, and the openness
                          and nothingness
leaving the frame
breaking the freeze frame——there will be no more flash backs

愛上虛擬情人

相思如雪花
抖落閃動的黑白
不在地上在心上
擾亂了高清的熒幕
你的面目糊了
哭笑拉成曲線
似有還無
我企圖伸手撫捉
電腦仍然溫熱
但鍵盤早已冷成一堆摩斯密碼
不肯吐露真情

甚麼時候喜歡都可以
隨便會面或道別
祇要打開電源
鍵入角色的名字
你必定依約前來
比情人準時
說鎖定的對白
走預設的刀光劍影
凝視鏡頭的所在
掛一個因果不變的微笑
這樣煽情的劇目
你我都演得生死與共
從搜狐到土豆
我們各在天涯的網絡
所思在遠道

In Love with a Virtual Lover

Yearning like snowflakes
shakes off the twinkling of black and white
not on the earth but in the heart
distorting the high-definition screen
your face is blurred
laughter and tears pulled and warped
like a return to nothingness
I try to catch it
the computer is tepid
and the keyboard has long since frozen into Morse code
unwilling to reveal the truth

Whenever you like is fine
you can come and go as you please
just flip the power on
type in the role's name
and you'll arrive as you promised
more punctual than a lover
for a canned conversation
with the preinstalled glint of cold steel
staring at the camera
putting on an unwavering smile
this rousing play
that we acted out holding nothing back
from sohu.com to tudou.com
we're both on the internet
and the one we love is far away

不在眼前
眼前祇剩下一堆死灰
人去如燈滅
這些年來他總蒼白無語
曾經抱住的身影
最後祇給我一個漂流的網址
承諾、問候
祇寄存於病毒的電郵
打從一個人開始愛上自己之後
便註定不同心　也離居
於是我把他的名姓和密碼
一拼按下消除

Not before our eyes
before our eyes is nothing but a pile of dead embers
people leave like a lamp clicking off
these past few years he's been pale and silent
and the form I once embraced
only gave me a website in the end
promises and best wishes
are sent in infected email
after one begins to love oneself
hearts will separate   and live apart
and so with one stroke
I delete his name and password

Interface

I.

你舞動你環抱空間
我書寫我刻鑿時間
就這樣邂逅發生了
撞成弧形的碎片
在0與1之間
散落或然率的四周

II.

左手交疊右手你把自己舞在其中
右腳交叉左腳我把聲光抱在其內
當音符悸動像逗點羞怯像虛線
我便知道心跳是圓形的
沒有出口

III.

你伸長指尖拉近視線的距離
在音樂節拍鎖住我的移動時
便向我走近

IV.

翻落地板的手和腳是一捆繩索
縛孤獨在這頭　迷失在那頭
纏繞燈光的絲線
我的眼睛從此迂迴曲折

Interface

I.

You dance your circumscribed space
I write my chiseled time
that was the way we happened to meet
fragments in splintered arcs
between 0 and 1
surroundings of scattered probability

II.

Left hand on right, you dance into the middle
right foot crossing over left, I hold my reputation between them
when the notes tremble like timid commas or a dotted line
I know that the heartbeat is a circle
and there is no way out

III.

You stretch out your fingers to draw the line of sight closer
when the rhythm of the music locks my movements
you come even closer

IV.

The hands and feet that fall to the ground are a coil of rope
tie loneliness up with that end   get lost in this end
bind up the strands of lamplight
from this point on my eyes run in circles

V.

暗下燈光以後便看不見你
祇有呼吸的氣聲擊落我的靜默

VI.

圓形的光圈內你給我笑臉
方框的燈區裏你給我背面
我祇好視而不見

VII.

當你在台上跟別人發生關連的時候
你柔動、你剛烈
我祇好軟癱成達利的時鐘
我敗死、我腐壞
愛與不愛便無能為力

V.

When the lights are dimmed I can no longer see you
the sound of breathing alone shoots down my silence

VI.

In the round aperture you show me a smiling face
in the square frame of the lamp you show me your back
I can only turn a blind eye

VII.

When you fall in love with someone on stage
you yield, you hold firm
I can only melt into one of Dali's clocks
I am slayed, I rot
powerless whether I love or not

一舞入魂

拐著高跟鞋來追風你的舞步
握著單程的票走迴旋的樓梯
被鎖住的凝望猶如兜轉的裙襬
踏亂了呼吸的次序
室內無風但我的思慮有一個黑洞
攪動的碎石如冰
哐啷哐啷的碰撞帶著透明的清脆
不能言說的一句話即將道破
如何才可免於落地對你的驚擾？
祇好將迷戀與迷亂擊成粉末　再散入
嘈嘈切切錯彈的視線

布幕拉起時你橫向的背立在
橢圓的燈區
閃著暈眩的紙屑從頂端灑落
如斷線的緣份極力抓住急降的飄離
墜落原是為了串連啊
如何才可免於命運的崩解？
旋起的氣流像纏繞的線
來自你曾經抱住的臂彎給我緊張的力度
琴音滑過鬆脫的空隙
你甩開拘禁的慾望讓四肢大開大合
翻成地上枝葉蔓延的動作
在沒有人愛沒有人的瓜葛裏
讓藤纏著瓜瓜纏著花

Spirit Dance

Turning in high heels to find your dancing
I grasp my one-way ticket up the escalator
my locked stare is like a spinning skirt
tapping out a panting rhythm
the room is airless but a black hole rests in my thoughts
where gravel churns up like ice
colliding with its transparent sharpness
what cannot be spoken is about to be revealed
how can I keep my landing from disturbing you?
Best to crush attraction and confusion   and scatter them
into the heady mix of notes.

When the curtain opens you have your back
to the oval spotlight
bright confetti sprinkles down from above
like broken fate trying to catch what's floating there
such falling was once meant to connect things
now how can it avoid disintegration?
The whirling air is like the tangled threads
of the nervous strength of your clinging arms
sound glides through the loosening gap
you lose the imprisonment of desire and let your limbs open and close
they translate into the spreading of leaves and branches
and in lovelessness and disassociation
vines entangle the melons and melons entangle the flowers

灰色的佈景不斷變換迷陣
走過起伏的線條你的身體
從這扇門隱沒那扇窗
從來無法分清左右
當你在台上我在台下的時候
不是鏡與影的依存
卻假想你在台上看得見
我在台下看著你在台上
彷彿祇有這種迂迴
我們才能如此親近

當影子疊著影子的時候
我們便跌入雙重黑暗
你在台上四面遊走尋找光源
我依舊被命定於觀眾席上
繼續曖昧不明
然後燈滅無聲
你的身影倏忽消失剎那帶來驚恐
會不會就這樣從此不見？
驟然你的舞影似箭
射入黑暗的盡頭
我便看見了光

當燈再亮時你原來仍在那裏
汗濕的背站在方形的燈區
守住一個等待的姿勢如銅牆鐵壁
不容眼神洞穿
也不允許掌聲擊潰
就這樣我和你對峙
直到騷動的人群靜止——

The gray scenery keeps changing its maze
of undulating lines and your body
disappears from this door to that window
always indistinct
when you're onstage and I'm in the audience
we're not a mirror and image that need each other to exist
still suppose that onstage you're watching
me in the audience watching you onstage
it seems like we
can only get close in this cycle

When shadows pile on shadows
we fall into double darkness
you walk across the stage and the light seeks you
I'm destined to stay in the audience
to be obscure
then the backlights go quiet
your sudden disappearance is terrifying
will you ever be seen again?
Suddenly your dancing shadow seems like an arrow
shooting out to the ends of the darkness
and I can see the light

When the lights come up you're still there
back wet with sweat and standing in a square of light
waiting like a fortress
not letting any gaze penetrate
not letting the applause affect you
so you and I face each other
until the crowd falls silent——

低沉的大提琴獨舞

我低沉得像大提琴的
無伴奏無聊得像
單簧管的獨腳戲
想你在舞中碎亂了頭髮與步法
便遺失了那飛擲的目力
當我不由自主地踏出鏡子的折射時
黑影從背後昇起網住了閃避的燈光
魍魎的飄蕩裏我的足尖
再也無法不倒在詛咒的斷音之間
你我的凝望剎那便啞了

甚麼時候你會給我一個回身
兩個托舉三個翻騰四個臂彎
當城市的石路支離破碎
空氣漲滿猜疑的塵蟎
我還可以不可以為了你的聲音
打很長途的電話然後跟你說無所事事
盛世的年華屬你我不能和你終老
才發現我們的時間差原來那麼致命

為了離你很近攫住那些單薄易散
暗角的影、冒犯的燈區
我決定繼續獨舞直到
大提琴和單簧管捨我而去

Solo Dance of a Low Cello

I am low as a cello
a cappella   ridiculous
as a clarinet going solo
I think of you dancing your hair and feet wild
then lose that projection
when I can't help but step before the mirror's reflection
shadows rise behind me to net the dodging light
the roving devils in my toes
now always end up among staccato curses
and when we stare at each other we turn mute

When will you give me a turn
two lifts   three somersaults   four arms
when the cobbled roads of the city are smashed
and the air swells with dust mites of suspicion
will I still be able
to call long distance just to hear your voice
this great era belongs to you   I can't grow old with you
only to discover that our age difference is fatal

To be close to you I seize feeble diffusions
shadows in dark corners, offending lights
I decide to keep dancing
until the cello and clarinet abandon me

NG舞台

使盡力氣學習蛇行與貓步
是為了離開你那細時好時壞的視線
當我再度走入燈光的位置
舞台的側面必然有風
呼吸氣若游絲
佈景的人祇好改變策略
臨時給我一堵虛假的牆
推開它　便碰撞了你
倒塌的支架裏愛情死無全屍

於是　燈光師摸黑尋找燈掣
服裝師在更衣室翻拾舞鞋
負責劇本的遺失了字詞
屈曲的指頭讓樂音啞了
我穿過空無觀眾的座位走向
亮著「出路」的黑洞
染色的長髮飄起像蛇
連自己都不能回顧
你嘶著含糊的語音叫嚷
──就這樣不顧而去嗎？
是的　因為墜落的水晶燈不是我懸掛的
被釘死的木窗不是我關閉的
連不能發聲的對白也不是我編撰的
既然你給我NG
我祇好拒絕重新開始！

The NG Stage

I try hard to learn a snake's slither and a cat's step
to leave the weave of your uneven sightlines
and when I cross into the spotlight
wind inevitably comes from the wings
my breath spins like gossamer
stagehands change their strategy
and put up a false wall for me
pushing past it   I bump into you
and inside the toppled trestle is love's mutilated corpse

And so   the lighting tech gropes for the light switch
the costume designer arranges dance shoes in the changing room
the one in charge of the script loses the words
a bent finger mutes the music
I pass through the empty audience seats
to the dark hole past the lit EXIT
long dyed hair floats up like snakes
and even I can't look back
at your muffled howls——
am I really going to leave like this?
Yes   because I wasn't the one who hung the falling chandelier
I wasn't the one who nailed the wooden window shut
I didn't even write the unspeakable dialogue
now that you've given me the NG Stage
all I can do is refuse to start over!

紅格子舞影

陽光畫著花臉潛入玻璃的時間
你的影子透明像風
黑色的膠地板斑駁了走近的舞步
有樹的手影在牆外招搖
你轉身旋繞的肩膊滑過半個弧形的圈
提腰與踢腿的急彎裏
紅格子的長褲網住了空間的輪廓
綿密地織著縱橫的線路
藏著停頓與起伏
讓音符與陰影穿越凝望
有時候昂首　有時候低頭

收起透明的風你向我問好
窗櫺一格一格的移動我們的影子
從門框、長廊、地磚直到斑馬線的黑白
傾斜四十五度的行人道上
你的聲線踏著琴鍵
我的視線拉著琴絃
當陽光和雨交織一起的時候
會是煙與火的蒸發嗎？
飛昇與下沉　爆裂或燃燒
當意志焚成曠野
城市失去所有路標
我仍會帶來一盞迷路的燈
照亮暗黑的舞影

A Shadow Dance of Red Checks

The sun paints its face and slips into the glass of time
your shadow is transparent as wind
the black rubber floor is stippled with approaching dance steps
the shadow puppets of trees show off outside
your spinning shoulders glide through a semi-oval
in the sharp turn of straight back and lifted legs
red-checkered pants ensnare the contours of the air
carefully weaving graceful lines
concealing the pauses, rises, falls
letting the notes and shadows cut across the gaze
at times head up   at times head bowed

Gathering the transparent wind you greet me
the window lattice moves our shadows inch by inch
from the door, corridor, and floor to the black and white
          stripes of the pedestrian crossing
on sidewalks slanted at forty-five degrees
your voice steps on piano keys
my vision plays on violin strings
when sunlight and rain mingle
will the smoke and fire evaporate?
flying and falling   bursting open or burning up
when willpower is burnt into a wilderness
the city will lose all its road signs
I will still carry a small lost lamp
to light up the dark shadows of dance

給飛蛾釘住旋轉的舞步

不要退——
你轉身背著鏡子向我
走步的說
我像被一隻飛蛾釘住了位置祇能
盯著鏡子裏你的背影
暈眩褪走四周閒人的閒語
祇有雷動的呼吸急促的旋轉再旋轉暈眩
耳畔很遙遠的角落我聽見針刺的聲音
便驟然驚醒
不分青紅皂白的退入沒有亮光的地方
你的肩膊垂下　視線黯淡
地面的距離逐漸拓大
浮躁在蔓延　靜默在收縮
頂端的燈光無端插入
鏡子和它的影子便開始動搖
彼此的拉鋸被迫在震央地帶
你扶著自己的心　我環抱自己的手
無言的聲軌剎那撞成心跳的死劫
空氣給填滿致命的二氧化碳
我們的步步為營與固步自封同時失陷了

失陷的天空無緣無故打開了一個缺口
清明過後雨水嘩啦嘩啦的一直像胃液倒流
斷魂路上積壓寸步難移的推搪
駛過的救護車響起無法救護的警號
我祇好閃避像一隻翅膀被打濕的飛蛾
沉重、衰竭卻盈滿奮力的虛脫

Choreography for a Pinned and Wriggling Moth

Don't pull away——
you turn around with your back to the mirror
and step toward me to say
I'm like a moth that's been pinned in place, and I can only
stare at your back in the mirror
dizzily pulling out of the easy chatter of people at ease
and there is only thunderous breath pulling me into turn after dizzying turn
in a corner far from my ears I hear a sound that pierces like a needle
and I wake up with a start
and tumble back into a place without light
your arms hang down   your sight dims
the distance on the floor gradually widens
restlessness spreads   the silence contracts
endless light inserts itself from above
the mirror and its reflection start to waver
pulling each other into the center in a tug-of-war
you hold up your heart   I encircle my hands
in an instant the silent soundtrack becomes the heart's death throes
the air is filled with fatal carbon dioxide
and our step-by-step movements and complacency fall to the enemy

The enemy-occupied sky breaches without reason
after it clears the sound of rain gurgles like stomach acid rising
the brokenhearted road back stores up stumbling excuses
a passing ambulance sounds a siren that can't save a thing
I can only dodge out of the way like a wet-winged moth
heavy, exhausted, and collapsed from its struggles

每次拍動對你的念想便移換了景物的排列
城市的軸心就這樣異變然後繼續公轉
直到我們無法再回到最初迷失的姿勢

甚麼時候你不再站在鏡子裏跟我說話
我便會翻開手掌讓你看看
因甜蜜而磨難的恐懼
如何裹成了繭　孵化成蛹
再風乾一路走來的碑石
當有一天歲月擊石成粉掌風碎了命運的線
你還願不願意為我
再旋轉一個舞步？

each time I touch my memory of you it changes the sequence of scenery
the axis of the city shifts weirdly and then continues to revolve
until we can no longer return to where we first lost our way

When the day comes you won't stand in the mirror to talk to me
I will open my hands to let you see
with sweet and suffering dread
how one becomes a cocoon   and hatches into a pupa
that tombstone that air dries on its journey
when time beats the stone to powder and the wind shreds fate's threads
will you still want to spin
a dance step for me?

遺落城市的瓶中舞

在弧線與虛線之間　不是直線
在地板與半空之中　不是橫切面
於是我們對望　卻看不見
我們說話　卻發不了聲
當視線與聲波被人群的干擾剪斷以後
我們用隱形的手語
填補空氣的破洞

橫臥你我之間有一道迴旋樓梯
鋒利的梯級割著封密的心事
容易踏空、滾跌於是步步驚心
人群像游離的魚不斷從身旁擦過
擦掉了肩膀碰撞的微音
擦花了猶豫停駐的回望
腳步像水流被陽光沖出門外
汽車剎那尖銳的響號
震亂了牆壁靜立的頻率
被僵住的表情祇留下一張空白的臉

「把舞步帶回家去吧！」臨別前你如是說
我把玻璃的話語裝入水瓶
搖動　讓它拍和節奏
靜止　讓它凝固軀體
然後帶著它流浪城市每個邊緣的起點
走一個圈子兩個方框無數的多邊形
放在長椅上擱在圓池旁或無形的荒境
在失語的狀態下穿過地車的森林

The Bottled Dance of a Lost City

Between an arc and an imaginary line   is not a straight line
between the floor and mid-air   is not a cross-section
so we look at each other   but see nothing
we talk   but make no noise
after our vision and voices are cut off by the crowd
we use hidden sign language
to fill in holes in the air

Between our prone bodies is a spiral staircase
sharp steps slice open private worries
it's easy miss to a step and fall terrified
the crowd brushes by us like floating fish
rubbing away the swish of shoulders on shoulders
rubbing out the memory of hesitant parking
the sunlight pushes a flow of feet out the door
and the sudden piercing honking of cars
wreak havoc with the walls' quiet frequency
deadlocked emotion leaves behind a white empty face

"Take the dance home!" You say this before we part
I put the specch of glass into a bottle.
when it moves   let it clap and beat
when it's still   let it solidify into a body
then let it rove from every starting point at the city limits
in a circle in two squares in countless polygons
put it on a bench or beside a round pond or in a shapeless wasteland
and when it is speechless let it pierce the forest of cars

巴士的海洋天橋的飛行道
直到走不下去倒在半途上
才打開瓶蓋將舞步釋放
還給你一個默劇的面具和一首寫不完的詩
裏面便是我全部的遺言——

the ocean of buses the flight-paths of overpasses
straight to the middle where there's nowhere left to go
before the bottle opens and lets the dance out
and returns a mime's mask to you and an unfinishable poem
and inside it will be my last will and testament

今夜燈光燦爛

銅鑼灣的晚上色光混纏像電視的屏幕
架起的路燈是鏡頭的眼睛
汽車喀嚓喀嚓的呼號像拉著菲林的軸輪
七色的光暈打印黝黑的柏油路上
拉出人潮左搖右擺的碎布衫影
因為旖旎所以給蒙上一層濡濕的薄膜
蠕蠕前行的鞋跟踢踏滿街的喁喁細語
泰式的熱飯混合日本湯麵的濃香令氣溫變壓
隱隱有一股辛辣有一分甜膩
路燈的鏡頭沿電車的鐵軌向前推移
和你走過拍賣下一季春裝的櫥窗
磨沙的玻璃折射我們側面凹凸的輪廓
走過二樓寵物店設在地面的招牌
平面的貓狗坐在廣告粗黑的標題上蠢蠢欲動
走過擺在水晶燈下的明星紙板公仔
那等量的身高甜美的笑容差點比我們更真實動人
最後和你坐在背景蒼白的茶餐廳內
你隨意叫來一碟沒有洋蔥的豬扒飯
那螢光的橙黃像一盤電影道具
於是你的手便顯得更纖瘦了
侍應給我送來一碗雲吞麵
雲吞像紙團麵條是橡皮筋
盤在碗裏開出永不凋謝的圖案
抬頭看見牆角有外露的電線紅綠相間
燈光照射不到的彎位有白色的蛛網
你從背包拿出日本買回來的科幻模型
紅色和綠色的塑膠模仿金屬的質感

The Lamplight Tonight Is Stunning

The colored lights at night at Causeway Bay Harbor entangle
               as though on a TV screen
the hung streetlamps are camera eyes
the wail of passing cars spools out like a roll of film
the dizzying colors of the spectrum imprint on the black asphalt
drawing out the crowd's reflected clothing on the wavering cloth
so luxuriant that it covers up a layer of wet film
heels wiggle forward and kick up a streetful of whispers
the smell of Thai rice and Japanese noodles electrifies the air
with hints of hot and oily sweet
the lenses of streetlamps follow the streetcar tracks
and the window you pass of a store selling clothes for the coming spring
the polished glass refracts our sides into concave and convex contours
passing a sign for the second floor pet shop
a 2D dog and cat sit on an advertisement's thick black captions waiting
               to make trouble
passing by a cardboard hero set under crystal lights
whose life-size sweet smile is almost more touching than ours
I finally sit down with you in a pallid teashop
you casually order pork-fried rice, hold the onion
like a movie prop under the glittering orange lights
your hand seems even thinner
the server brings me a bowl of wonton soup
the wontons are like balls of paper and the noodles are rubber bands
that coil in the bowl to reveal an immortal pattern
I lift my head and see alternating red and green wires in a corner
in a curve beyond the reach of the light is a white spider web
you take an action figure bought in Japan from your bag
the red and green plastic mimics the feel of metal

褪色的肢體伸延它年月的價值
原來我們的城市連玩具也流行「古著」
刻意的磨損連帶感情也是最時尚的款式
我放下手中的模型依舊專注的吃麵
盤結的麵條在胃裏搞起星球大戰
然後你給我從台北故宮買來的文具
便條、文件夾和記事簿都印上畢加索的名畫
總是一個女人兩種面向的頭顱
不斷的圈圈來來回回像巡視的眼睛
搜尋可供盯緊的對象
我放下厚重的顏色又拿起輕巧的線條
動作的起落間瞥見你一張凝固的臉沒有言語
——甚麼時候走呢?
——明天。
這時候室內的燈光有點暗下來了
眼前的桌椅、杯盤和你都無法對焦
站起身來你走向柜枱結賬
是的,該是離去的時候了夜這樣傾斜
但我依然眷戀安穩不變的座位
因為擺動的街景下
今夜的燈光這樣燦爛

as the limbs fade it will stretch its annual value
in our city even toys are popular "retro" objects
the most fashionable kind are well-worn and well-loved
I put the figure down and go back to my soup
the coiled noodles begin their own Star Wars
next you hand me some stationary from the imperial palace in Taipei
a notepad, a folder, a notebook—all printed with famous Picassos,
invariably a woman with a head facing in two directions
endlessly circling examining eyes
searching for a target to stare at
I put down the heavy color and pick up a light line
and as I move I glimpse your hardened speechless face
——When do you leave?
——Tomorrow.
At that moment the room darkens slightly
the table and chairs, the glasses and plates, and you go out of focus
you stand up and go to pay the bill
yes, it must be time to leave and night tilts in
but I still cling to my solid chair
because under the swaying street scene
the lamplight tonight is stunning

給電腦的情書

滿以為很瞭解你因為
跟你這樣朝夕相對呼吸相連
已經三年零十個月了
我的姓名、性別、履歷和理想
通通分類存檔並且定期更新
任滑鼠隨時進入或下載
你都給我無限寬容或寬頻
遊歷於上下合縱左右連橫的空間
你輕盈的樂聲總吻合我跳躍的舞步
跳出情感互動的一片藍幕
（藍幕的下角有青草
上角有小花和恐龍）
原以為可以和你白頭到老永結同心
一如酒樓菜牌上紅底金字的承諾
但原來你也有背叛的時刻
偷偷跟旁人搭訕然後搭線而且
還很小心地讓我讀到你們的情話與暗碼
於是我開始猜疑你花亂而閃爍的面容
暴力敲打鍵盤上每個凹凸可疑的指模
或用苦纏的動作拉扯已經鬆脫的電線
期求你不再板起冷漠的凝視
對我輸入的話語不聞不問
或隨意亂碼顧左右而言他
甚至突然自動關機從此不再跟我會面
是的　沒有受過專業訓練的我
並不能熟練地操作戀愛的各種程式

Love Letter to a Computer

I thought I knew you because
all night and day our breath mingles together
for three years and ten months
my name, gender, resumé, and ideas
have been classified as files and updated at the set time
entered or downloaded according to the mouse
you've given me unlimited broadmindedness and broadband
to traverse the up/down left/right horizontal/vertical space
your lovely musical voice accompanies my dancing
your blue screen quits out of emotional interactions
(there's grass in the lower corner of the screen
in the upper corner there are tiny flowers and dinosaurs)
I used to think we would grow old together
like in the promises of a red and gold menu
but you've had your moments of betrayal
secretly conversing with others and making contacts
but also carefully letting me read your intimate notes and codes
until I began to suspect your unruly flickering face
pounding the keyboard with all my suspicious fingers
or bitterly pulling on the loose cords
I pray you won't ever stare blankly at me again
ignoring every word I type
or casually change the subject to code
until you suddenly shut down and refuse to see me
yes, since I have no special training
I can't just skillfully make various attachments

——密碼錯誤，請重新輸入
　（你說過會一輩子待我好
　　無論我們是甚麼但那
　　「甚麼」到底是甚麼？）
——程式偏差，無法存檔
　（我們曾經一起吃飯的
　　那間茶餐廳因為
　　樓宇遷拆而倒閉了）
——網頁無法啟動，請稍候
　（當我打算在你的電子郵箱留下
　　口訊時你剛巧致電到我的傳真機
　　彼此的網絡因為佔線而阻斷）
——線路繁忙，請按Refresh
按下去突然一屋暗燈
牆壁發出陣陣燒焦的惡臭
當神經線錯接電腦系統時才發現
自己原來是個電腦與愛情白痴
——「懂得愛戀自己的人才得享永生！」
上帝（如果有的話）也禁不住竊笑然後搖頭嘆息
為我這句史無前例的盟誓

——Wrong password, please try again
      (you said you would wait for me your whole life
      no matter what but what does that
      "what" really mean?)
——ERROR, your file has not been saved
      (we used to eat together
      but that café closed
      when the building was torn down)
——This page cannot be opened, please try again in a moment
      (just as I planned to send you an email
      you sent a message to my fax machine
      and with the line busy, neither one could go through)
——The line is currently busy, please refresh the page
and when I refresh it things suddenly go dark
the wall lets off an acrid stench of burning
and when I mistakenly connect my nerves to the system I realize
I was an idiot when it came to computers and love
——"Only those who understand love will live forever!"
even God (if there is) has to snicker and sigh
over this unprecedented oath of alliance.

飛天棺材

凌晨五時被雷聲劈醒
醒來第一句想跟你說的話
是我們的算計都錯誤了

房子外面有一條公路
公路上有一種飛天棺材
棺材內的十六條性命
祇交給一個司機
如果他不喝酒、不抽煙、不談手提電話
如果天不下雨、不長霧
路邊不閃出小狗或老人
我相信是可以長命富貴的
常常在亡命的旅途上
聽同一首歌哼重覆的拍子
每次歌詞昇到最高的音節時
車子總剛巧滑過一個死亡的彎角
車輪傳來撕裂的呼喊
拋出愛情的離心力使人虛脫
於是便記起凌晨五時雷聲的警號
我們真的無路可走嗎?

假日的時候公路總堵滿車子
像無頭無尾的彩色蜈蚣
彎彎曲曲的關節兩頭都不是結局或開始
沿路有警察維持或干預秩序
卻無法改善寸步難移的局面
當路途因外來的擠壓而變得踟躕的時候
是不是該放棄原地踏步呢?

The Flying Coffin

Woken by thunder at five in the morning
the first thing I want to tell you
is that all of our plans have gone wrong

Outside our building is a highway
on the highway is a flying coffin
inside the coffin are sixteen lives
all handed over to the driver
if he doesn't drink or smoke or talk on his cell phone
if it doesn't rain or turn foggy
if no dogs or old people suddenly appear in the road
I believe we will lead long and full lives
on these desperate escapes
I listen to the same song and hum along
each time the song rises to its highest pitch
the minibus swerves by a deadly corner
the wheels squeal
people collapse in the centrifugal force of lost love
and so I remember the thunder's warning before dawn
do we really have no way out?

On holidays the highway is one big traffic jam
like a colorful centipede with neither head nor tail
the zigzagging links at either extreme are neither the beginning nor end
along the way the police do their best
but there's no improving an impossible situation
the pressure builds into indecision
should we abandon the gridlock?

當後面的車子不耐煩地碰撞前面的時候
是不是該設法逃離現場呢？
鐳射唱片的音樂依舊流動
沒有因天氣、距離或交通事故而停頓
然而
愛冒險的小巴司機突然也會心血來潮
在危急關頭考驗闖過黃燈的速度
剎時撞向石壆再反彈鐵欄
才發現連唱盤也會跳針電源也會中斷
原來相愛很難
當你在公路的那頭我在這頭的時候

沿路有甚麼風景　我們
便祇可選擇怎樣的窗口
從天橋到地面
從來都不是一個踏實的轉向
我們以為平放地上的
會比懸盪空中的易於掌握
卻不知道半空的視線才可
鳥瞰路面的全景
祇是風景的切換太快
在來不及記認每個細節之前
你已經在相反的車線上跟我再見

凌晨五時從黑洞醒來才記起
我們的愛情
是開在公路上的飛天棺材
隨時會死在半途上

When a car hits the one in front
should it flee the scene?
The CD's music flows like before
not pausing for the weather or distance or accident
even so
the reckless minibus driver is suddenly seized by a whim
to speed up at a critical juncture
and in an instant strikes the curb and bounces back to the railing
with the skip of the disc and cut power I realize
how hard it is to love one another
when you're at one end of the highway and I'm at the other

What we see along the way
is determined by which window we choose
from the overpass to the road
no direction has ever been dependable
we thought that being on the ground
would be easier than being suspended in the sky
but we didn't realize we would only get
a bird's-eye view of everything in midair
it all happened so quickly
and before there was a chance to remember details
you were saying goodbye from the opposite lane

Only waking from the abyss of five o'clock did I remember
that our love
is a flying coffin speeding down the highway
and at any moment it can hit a dead end

感情幹線

Sometimes the snow comes down in June
Sometimes the sun goes 'round the moon
Sometimes 我和你分叉
城市高危吊詭的幹線

每當列車隆隆駛入月台的剎那
漆黑的隧道總會空白一片
沒有血色的玻璃門上注滿
一雙一對鬼影幢幢的眼睛
看不透門外蠕動的風景
除了努力抓緊一根金屬的扶手外
我們別無他法制止
情感迅速的滑落

無論踏入還是踏出車廂
我們都不能逃避月台的跨越
無論是追、趕、跑、跳
這一步原是無可厚非的
讓中途的路程提前圓滿
但往往祇有「請勿超越黃線」
或「小心月台空隙」的警告
霸佔你我密集擠塞的思維
唯是欠缺這個姿勢
我們終於也無法行行重行行了

Tracks of Emotion

Sometimes the snow comes down in June
Sometimes the sun goes 'round the moon
Sometimes we diverge
on the city's strange and dangerous tracks

When each train roars into the station
a section of the pitch-black tunnel turns blank
the color-drained glass door fills
with pair after pair of ghostly sparkling eyes
that can't see through to the scene creeping by
aside from grasping onto the metal handles
we have no way of stopping
our emotions from quickly slipping by

No matter how we step in or out of the train
we have to cross the platform gap
whether chasing, catching up, running, jumping
it is a blameless step
that cuts a successful journey in half
but there are often warnings "Please do not cross the yellow line"
or "Be mindful of the gap"
our thoughts are crammed with them
but we still lack that mindset
and in the end we can't go on or start again

把最好的都留在最後
管它是月台還是舞台
毋須送我回家
也不打算眷顧你流連的背影
就讓兩邊相反相成的隧道
同時響起列車開動的噪音
那時候期待　你依然相信
Sometimes the snow comes down in June
Sometimes the sun goes 'round the moon
Sometimes 我和你分叉
兩條終極無間的感情線

Leave the best for last
whether on the platform or stage
there's no need to see me home
I won't be tender toward your parting shadow
let the tunnels on either side
ring with the simultaneous noises of two trains starting up
then with hope   you still believe
Sometimes the snow comes down in June
Sometimes the sun goes 'round the moon
Sometimes we diverge
on the city's strange and dangerous tracks

負離子情人

為了改掉眷戀你的劣根性
決定到髮型屋做一個完美的
負離子直髮

坐在鏡前
你的影像一閃而過
鏡子便因螺絲的鬆脫而擺動
皺著眉我讓身軀下沉
椅子因無法承載想你的重量
而吱吱作響
染金髮的女孩拿著電板
在我的頭上挑起燙熱的慾望
髮絲越拉越長
長長久久的伸向你居住的城市
卻又抵受不住地心吸力的拉扯
而纏結扭動
女孩的動作凝在空中
是四分一音符的慢鏡停格
你的鏡像鬼魅般閃過
瞬間再有分叉的髮梢枯黃和折斷
當冷風機呼呼開動的時候
落了滿地斷髮呼痛你的名字

廣告說負離子能使受傷損的秀髮
再生　而且柔順、守時和靜默
那大概是負負得正離別再重聚的結果吧
但我並沒有多餘的頭髮可以捨掉贈你

Ion Lover

To rid myself of you
I decide to go to the salon for perfectly
ion-straightened hair

Sitting in front of the mirror
your image flashes by
the mirror's screws are loose and it begins to sway
I sit back frowning
the chair can't bear the weight of my thoughts of you
and begins to creak
a girl with dyed-blonde hair holds a flat iron
and burning desires spring from my head
each strand is pulled longer and longer
stretching toward the city where you live
but they can't withstand gravity's pull
and tangle up again into writhing curls
the girl's movements solidify in the air
like stop-motion quarter notes
your image flashes by like a ghost
and in an instant my split ends wither and break
when a cold breeze whips up
the hair that covers the ground painfully exhales your name

The ad said ion-straightening can bring damaged hair
back to life   it's gentle, quick and quiet
it's the shameful result of splitting up and getting back together
but I don't have much extra hair to give up for you

到底留頭還是留髮
留長、留短還是蜚短流長
祇關乎個人臉形的選擇
跟關關雎鳩無關

剪掉多餘的思念
離棄沉溺的坐椅
走出竊竊私語的髮型屋
推開凝定的玻璃門
把黑白的眉目甩回牆上的掛曆
迎向陽光刺眼的方向
揚起的直髮和視線
帶來了風的顏色

於是
你再也無法尋回
帶著負離子出走的情人

should I let my hair grow or keep it styled
leave it long or short, or neither long nor short
is a question of the shape of a person's face
and has nothing to do with romance

Trim off all the unnecessary longings
leave that squishy chair
walk out of the whispering salon
open the sticking glass door
toss all black and white logic back at the calendar
face the dazzling sun
and your flowing straight hair and line of sight
bring in the wind's colors

And so
you have no way to recover
that lover who took away the ions

愛人・衣服

期待有兩個夏季
可以延長愛情的定期儲蓄
期待愛人如衣服
隨每天的潮流更新想念的姿態

三月的霧和雨連成一線
特意披一件波希米亞的通花上衣
讓袖口的絲縫起兩座城市的間隙
剪成郵票錯體相連的齒痕
四月的太陽有一張陰陽的臉
驟雨中的彩虹配一條紫水晶的蝴蝶結
讓磁場拍和心跳的振率
相信及時拉住你亂闖馬路的手
有恆久拍翼的能量
五月的夜有星星洞穿了的天
小心翼翼塗上閃金的唇彩
描出蛇的眉額在街燈的映照下
你的眼睛印下我的影子

然後六月和八月都過去了
吵罵的七月給我們遺失或遺忘
是時候把過時的衣服好好殮藏
分門別類再分道揚鑣
see through 的雪紡仍看不透你去留的心思
牛仔褲的流蘇拉得太長變成糾纏的負累
田園的印花吹不開一個愛情綠色的結局
刺繡的民族圖案不過是騙人的不老傳說

Lovers * Clothes

I look forward to two summers
that prolong love's expiration date
I look forward to lovers that like clothes
follow new styles and renew longing

The fog of March threads into the rain
throwing on a patterned Hermès jacket
sewing the gaps between two cities with its silken sleeves
until they're like the tooth-mark links between postage stamps
the April sun's *yinyang* face
the rainbows from sudden rainstorms match an amethyst butterfly knot
give in to the magnetic pulsing and the heart's rhythm
and belief will quickly grasp onto your wild dashing hand
with the energy of persistent flapping wings
on May nights the stars pierce the sky
carefully wing-brushing on sparkling gold lipstick
under the light of streetlamps, eyebrows form snakes
and your eyes imprint my shadow

Then June and August are gone
and cursing July brings loss or forgetting
it's time to encoffin our outmoded clothing
to classify and cull
see-through lace can't see through whether you'll stay or go
jeans tassels are pulled into tangled complications
pastoral prints can't offer love a pleasant green result
embroidered folk designs are fakes instead of traditional

去年流行的服飾今年已成舊人
今年緊緊抱住的身影無法過渡
明年春季的花生騷
原來拋棄一件衣服或給潮流甩掉
並不如想像中困難
原來愛人如衣服
曾經緊貼然後冷卻是體溫
因汗漬而斑駁
別人還會說三道四
說衫長褲短衣不稱身呢
如果我有兩個夏季
會重新選擇愛情的起點
因為七月是我出生的日子
而你總會刻意忘記
其實某年冬天你生日的時候
曾偷偷給你放下一條灰領巾

last year's popular styles have already become old lovers
the figures that this year holds onto can't be ferried over
to next year's springtime Fashion Show
but throwing away clothing or casting off a fad
isn't as hard as it seems
lovers and clothing
what was once so tight and then cooled off is body temperature
mottled with sweatstains
and still some will gossip
saying the shirts and pants and shorts don't fit
if I had two summers
I would choose the beginning of love
because I was born in July
which you always deliberately forgot
though one winter on your birthday
I secretly set aside a gray scarf for you

我在美白的日子

我在美白的日子
謝絕探訪
因為怕光
便不能應付朋友閃亮的鏡片
那同情和諒解
自以為灼熱
其實最會殺死正在更生的細胞

最近由於戀愛
所以患上了黑斑過敏症
那是一種會隨年月
而衰老的情愛
而且深入皮膚的內層
任算天然海底植物提煉的磨砂
也磨不掉的
一生的印記

聽說SKII有剝殼雞蛋的面膜
可以二十四小時再生暗啞的傷口
祇要循環使用二十八天
一心一意的信任和等候
你總會帶著在外面因遊蕩
而老去的容顏回來
可是我天生對雞蛋敏感
而且無法釋懷雞與蛋先後的次序
終於也搞不清楚應該

On Skin-Whitening Days

On skin-whitening days
I politely refuse to go out
because I'm afraid of the light
and can't handle my friends' glittering lenses
their sympathy and understanding
seems scorching
when what actually kills is in the midst of multiplying cells

Because of love I've recently
developed allergic dark spots
it's a kind of passion
that ages over time
and embeds deep in the skin
a bit of sand polished by seafloor flora
can't rub away
a lifetime of lines

I've heard SK-II makes a facial mask from peeled eggs
and in twenty-four hours it can heal mute dark wounds
it needs to cycle for twenty-eight days
and with wholehearted trust and patience
you can rejuvenate a face
grown old from its travels
but I was born with a sensitivity to eggs
and I can't forget the question of the chicken and egg
and finally I'm not sure if I should

跟你相戀然後分手還是
先分手才再相戀
於是最後決定這兩個護膚程序
同一時間進行

當然
我並不想真的
把你看成無藥可救的黑頭或粉刺
因為深層的潔淨和漂白
會帶來切膚之痛
但在不能換臉的情勢下
祇好戒掉對你的念念不忘

我在美白的日子
長高了一英寸　長胖了兩公斤
不再失眠、厭食和怠倦
皮膚懂得飲水
思源　明白愛慕自己
可以去除皺紋和暗瘡
讓陽光帶來小鳥的歌唱

love you first and then break up or
first break up and then love you again
so finally I decide that both of these skin-protective sequences
should be carried out simultaneously

Of course
I don't really want
to see you as incurable blackheads or acne
since deep cleaning and bleaching
will bring skin-rending pain
but since I can't change my face
I can only give up thinking about you

On skin-whitening days
I grow an inch   I gain two kilos
with no more insomnia or lack of appetite or listlessness
the skin knows
its origins   it knows how to love itself
it can dislodge wrinkles and dark veins
and let the sun usher in birdsong

兩個阿當

然後有了光
我便看見
有兩個阿當

伊甸園在經濟滑落後倒閉
能夠變賣的都已經化作春泥
蛇帶腹語術與無花果
移民沒有地震的地方
上帝為了懲罰背叛的夏娃
把阿當一分為二

左面的阿當流落城北
用耳朵聽風的歌聲
右面的阿當住在城南
用眼睛攝錄山水的顏色
從一九九六到二〇四六
他們仍在守候
夏娃隨著板動的地殼前來相認
然而　風和水仍各不相干
山和路也互不虧欠
左青龍　右白虎
中間一個昏睡的夏娃
秋涼時一個月光
元宵的佳節兩串鞭炮
清明的墳上便有三炷清香

Two Adams

Then there was light
and I saw
there were two Adams

The Garden of Eden went bankrupt in the economic collapse
all that could be sold off turned to fertile soil
the snake brought figs and ventriloquism
and immigrants to places without earthquakes
to punish Eve the traitor
God split Adam in two

Adam's left side wandered north of the city
and listened to the song of the wind
Adam's right side lived south of the city
and memorized the landscape
from 1996 to 2046
they were waiting
for Eve to follow the earth's moving crust and find them
but the wind and water weren't connected
the mountains and roads weren't indebted to each other
on the left a green dragon   on the right a white tiger
in the middle a sleepy Eve
a moonbeam in the autumn chill
two strips of firecrackers for the Lantern Festival
three joss sticks for graves on Tomb Sweeping Day

當城市的回歸由紀念
變成悼念的時候
你已經離家五年了
而他　卻再度造訪我的家門
房子的鈴聲因日久失修而啞了
無法搖響舊日或以後的誓言或遺言
於是音樂從歌聲的身上脫落
風景從鏡頭的眼睛失去視線
我們再也回不了家

曾經以為
帶著新的護照便可以
從頭開始生活的旅程
但走過了歷史的圈和套才發現
我們在彼此的時差裏搞錯了方向
門被掩上之後
便再也無法交疊觸碰的身影

期待另一次洪荒
讓頹垣敗瓦把你們二合為一
或由熊熊烈火帶來另一個夏娃
因為沒有誰能逃得過蛇的咀咒
當智慧變成負擔
我們便錯過了愛情

By the time the city's handover memorial
had turned to mourning
you'd been gone five years
but he   still came to call at my door
the doorbell was mute from so many years of disuse
and couldn't ring out the old days or oaths that came after
so music was separated from singing
and the scenery lost the eye of the camera
we can never go home again

We once thought
with new passports we could
start a new life
but passing through the sheath and cycle of history we realized
with the time difference that we'd gone in the wrong direction
after the door was shut
we couldn't pile up all of the forms we'd touched

Expect another prehistoric period
let the ruined walls and tiles combine you two into one
or from the raging flames bring forth another Eve
because no one escapes the snake's curse
when wisdom became a burden
we began to miss out on love

解體

在未曾看清便已經厭倦的速度裏
我們該如何趨吉
和避凶呢？

新年有許多生肖和星座的運程預測
你和我被界分十二個種類
各自抱住不同的吉星和凶險
以單腳站立的姿勢
企在圓形的冰面上
這時候我真的無法想像你的臉
會是一個刻滿花紋的羅盤
隨環境的磁場旋轉你意志的方向
旋起漫天桃花的落瓣
我知道你並不希罕空間的捕捉
戴上屬龍或山羊座的符號也不過是
為了方便逃逸
在飛天和遁地之間其實
天地已給我留下缺口
一線僅容半隻手掌探索的命脈
伸出五指我還給自己
無法逃離掌心的指紋
假裝生有時死有時
愛情有時——

然後電視新聞傳來
穿梭機在空中解體的聲音
預示我們的年代將無可避免
在左搖右擺中渡過

Disintegration

At this exhausting incomprehensible speed
how can we bring about good fortune
and avoid disaster?

Plenty of Chinese zodiac and horoscope predictions are made at New Years
you and I are divided by twelve signs
each brings a different kind of luck and danger
standing on one leg
in the ice rink
I can't imagine your face
as a compass engraved with patterns
that spins your will according to the magnetic fields
I know you don't care about capturing space
and putting on a dragon symbol or Capricorn
is merely a convenient way to escape
between flying and burrowing
the universe has left me an opening
a thin lifeline barely big enough for half a palm
stretching out five fingers I take back
the fingerprints that can't escape the hand
and pretend there's a time for life and a time for death
a time for love——

And then the TV news comes on
the sound of the space shuttle disintegrating
predicts our inescapable fate
tossed by the tides

我寧願相信那些星塵
有你無重的軌跡
丁點丁點的灑落
糖果盤上已經冷卻的祝願
而新年也就這樣變舊了

I prefer to believe that stardust
will follow your weightless orbit
and sprinkle down bit by bit
the good wishes in the candy bowl have gone cold
and just like that the new year turns old

戀戀風SARS

從此你我必須相隔三呎距離
從此我要戴上口罩跟你說話
從此我們不能握手祇可道別
直到我的身體對你非典型的情愛
產生免疫的抗體為止

四月的季候風慵懶、羞澀而且兇猛
帶來城市疫症的花粉並且蔓延
你電郵決絕的病毒
打開窗戶如同打開死亡的溝渠
我無法辨認站在二十四樓的高度
當摯愛的歌手用飄落的身影
糊住生命的視線
我對你原有的思念便嘭然中斷
零碎四散的雨點擊在欄杆上
原來
真的
很痛

在風和它的沙和SARS戀戀廣播的日子
小島的燈火因虛怯而浮腫和無眠
閉上眼睛我聽見
長途電話另一端你的歌聲
急促的呼吸斷續的言詞
卡在哽咽的喉鼻間便無可挽回
告訴你家中的小貓病了
我們隨時會死在隱瞞的病變裏
你說時間過了限期

The Loving Wind and SARS

From now on we keep three feet apart
from now on I wear a surgical mask to talk with you
from now on we can't hold hands, just say goodbye
until my body's peculiar love for you
stops producing antibodies

The monsoons of April are sluggish, shy, but fierce
they bring a pestilence of pollen to the city that extends
to the virus that shut down your email
to open a window is to open a canal of death
I don't know the height of the twenty-fourth floor
but when my beloved singer fluttered down
it blurred life's eyesight
and the longing I felt for you was over abruptly
scattered raindrops strike the railings
and as a matter of fact
it really
hurts

These days the wind and sand broadcast SARS
the island's lights are weak, swollen and sleepless
I close my eyes and hear
your singing on the other end of the long distance call
your words are interrupted by gasps
they get caught in your throat with sobs and are lost forever
I tell you my kitten is sick
we could die anytime from some hidden illness
you say your time is up

敏感的城市總會積壓抑鬱的基因
無可避免無一倖免
放下話筒躺在床上直到清晨六時
閉塞的天空始終無法亮起
一個呼吸暢順的早晨
想到有一天
當我對你不再提防免疫的時候
或許我們便可除下N95的障礙
點頭、微笑、再分道揚鑣
從此、
然後——

a depressive gene overwhelms this sensitive city
unavoidable, inescapable
I hang up and lie in bed until six in the morning
the heavy sky doesn't brighten
a morning of easy breathing
I think of a day
when I'll no longer be on guard against infection
maybe we can take off our N95 barriers
and nod, smile, and part again
from now on,
and after——

溜在冰上的墓誌銘

我真的無法輕省柔順的
控制自己的身體在冰面上
至死方休地旋轉
而旋轉
衹是為了終止

如果成長等於蒼老
何時？
讓我變身懷面超人
而變身的動作
就是原地踏步
用旋轉的風景
模糊前世今生的刮痕和磨損
於是我舉起前臂
原地急速的打圈
直到力盡的時候才可以
將青春剎住

白色的冰面上前一個圓
後一個圓
是教練俯身用藍筆
給我畫下的規範
穿上四號的冰鞋
我必須用前後的交叉步
回回來來圓圈與圓圈之間的距離
堅冰無固
水痕無我

Epitaph on Ice

There's no graceful way
to control my body on the ice
spinning in a death spiral
and I have to spin
just to come to a stop

If growing up equals growing old
when will it happen?
Let me be reborn as the Masked Rider
and the transformation
is like marching in place
the spinning scene
obscures the wear and tear of the last life on this one
so I lift my arms
to make faster circles
and only when I'm completely exhausted can I
put the brakes on youth

There's a circle on the ice in front of me
and a circle behind me
drawn by my instructor
to guide me
I put on size four skates
and do a cross-step
around the circles and between them
ice has no form
water traces have no self

交叉的腳步總常常行差踏錯
不是飛出了圓周的外弦便是
陷入進退維谷的中央
年輕的教練有時候企圖
伸手把我拉回來
但離心的力量太過義無反顧
死硬的軀體總會朝相反的方向跌下

躺在冰面上其實有一種安祥
跟死亡的觸感一樣跳動的溫度
逐漸融化長期站立的酸痛
當無須再伸長脖子掙扎仰視
來年是否歲月靜好的時候
我便知道
這就是所謂「終止」！

my cross-steps frequently go astray
and instead of flying along the thin circumference
I sink into the center of the pit
the young instructor sometimes tries
to catch me and pull me back
but the centrifugal forces are too strong
and my stiff body always falls away

Lying on the ice is somehow comforting
like the dead I feel the pulsing cold
melt away the ache of standing too long
there's no need to crane my neck to look up
whether or not next year is a good one
I know
this is what is called "the end"!

鼻敏感之戀

患上了鼻敏感便注定
不得不對你杯弓蛇影
當然
蛇會在冰天雪地裏冬眠
而在這人造的溜冰場上
你祇會鳳舞九天

滑行在你的後面
可以輕而易舉的看到
你黑色的背影輪廓分明
企立在你的面前
總常常低頭便無法瞧見
你眼睛和鼻子的距離

牽著我的手你教我
從側面跳到背面去
緊緊盯著自己的鞋面
我差點以為自己是一隻金色的鳳凰
可以隨意的飛上枝頭
誰知道失重的盤算
險些讓自己的前額親吻冰地
你閃出右手及時拉住倒下的肩膊
我的手肘大意地撞向你的腰間
你問我為甚麼手心發抖
很想告訴你不是因為寒冷
也不是因為剛才險象環生

Allergic Love

Those burdened with allergies are destined
to be jittery near you, like near a snake
of course
snakes will sleep underneath the snowy ground in winter
but on the artificial skating rink
you can only spin into a phoenix rising to the sky

Skating behind you
it's easy to see
your distinctive dark shadow
and standing on tiptoe in front of you
I often lower my head so I can't see
the distance between your eyes and nose

You hold my hand and teach me
how to jump back from one side
staring closely down at my shoes
I almost believe I'm a golden phoenix
who can fly onto a branch at any moment
but who can calculate weightlessness
and I nearly kiss the ice with my forehead
in a flash you catch my shoulder with your right hand
my elbow carelessly hits your waist
you ask me why my hands are shaking
and I want to say it isn't because of the cold
and it isn't because the danger just passed

你挺直身子再示範
一氣呵成如水銀瀉地的動作
模仿你的步法我依舊左搖右擺
你把笑容壓在冰面下
拉開我的前臂然後逆時針的轉圈
方形的冰場頓時變成圓形的暈眩
冷風觸動你的和我的衣袖
你要我抬頭直視前面的方向
但你就在我的跟前擋去了視線
我祇好急忙地把你的和我的腳步同時剎住

患上了鼻敏感空氣中難免
有多餘的水份
很想對你的話語和偶爾的笑聲
打一個史無前例的噴嚏
但為了不想驚動室內的溫度和濕度
我把噴嚏轉喻為優雅的點頭
你皺著眉問我到底明白不明白
我拼命的忍住呼吸但鼻酸帶來了淚水
你轉身輕輕的嘆息然後把我拉到欄杆處
才發現
你的掌心比我冰冷

You straighten up and demonstrate again
your smooth movements like spilling quicksilver
I lurch back and forth trying to imitate
and you keep your smile pressed beneath the ice
you draw back my arm and turn me counterclockwise
the rectangular rink becomes a dizzying circle
a cold wind stirs our sleeves
you want me to lift my head to look forward
but you're blocking my line of sight
I can only hastily stop my feet the moment you do

In the fresh air, those who suffer from allergies
can't help but overproduce fluids
and with you talking and occasionally laughing I really want
to let loose an incredible sneeze
but because I don't want to disturb the warmth and humidity inside
I turn the sneeze into a graceful dip of my head
you wrinkle your brows and ask me if I understand
I try not to breath but the tickling in my nose makes me tear up
you turn around to sigh and pull me over to the railing and only then
do I realize your hands are even colder than mine

當城市蒼老的時候

當這個城市開始蒼老
我們還可以年輕多久?

回歸的晚上
到處是煙花的幻影
散落於城市每一張臉孔
浮游、明滅而零零瑣瑣
幽冷的你陪著蒼白的我走過
一段蜿長、曲折而傾斜的路
催促的車聲、沸騰的人群
喀嚓喀嚓從身邊掠過
猶如失落的煙火
把美豔的繁華都拖在背後

下過雨的台階
有幢幢濕滑的倒影
蘭桂坊的酒香
舞旋於燃著點點霓虹的星空
有柔軟的歌聲從擠擁的角落冒起
參予節目的人互相擁抱和祝福
走在你的背後
我低頭避開簷蓬的雨水
卻看見一張裝飾的布幔
飄起你單薄的身影
推開四方八面的人潮
抱著冬夜一般墨藍的沉默與寒意
我追趕你前行的腳步
輕微的雨花瀟瀟灑灑
視線罩起了一層煙霞

When the City Gets Old

When this city starts to get old
how long can we stay young?

The night of the handover
fireworks were everywhere
scattering over every face in the city
ephemeral, flickering and gone
on our walk you were cold and remote, I was wan
on the winding slanted road
the impatient cars and seething crowds
zoomed past us
like falling firecrackers
dragging their extravagant beauty behind them

The rain-drenched steps
flickered with wet reflections
a smell of alcohol from Lan Kwai Fong
whirled with the burning neon in the sky
soft singing seeped out from the crowded corners
revelers embraced and wished each other well
walking behind you
I lowered my head to avoid the rain from the canopies
and watched your patterned cloak
flapping about your thin form
people streamed in every direction
in the silence and chill of an ink-blue winter night
I followed your footsteps
a light rain pitter-pattered down
misting over my eyes

刹那間我竟無從確認
這城市與你
真實的輪廓

假如這城市已經衰老
我們還可以年輕多久？

午夜十二時過後
聽說是另一個時代的開始
路邊有打翻的酒瓶
碎裂的玻璃折射幽暗的綠光
我們停步、回頭
搜尋來時的風景
空空洞洞的風颳起無處歸落的髮梢
靠近你的身旁
聽醉漢的歌聲寥落一條黑漆的冷巷
熱鬧在街的另一頭響起
我們該如何走過這世紀的路程？

世紀的旅程
以節目的嘉年華開始
豔紅、輝煌而喜氣洋洋
有人穿起了民族的服飾舞動一條
還未睡醒的金龍有人拉起了咿啞的胡琴奏出
吞吞吐吐的樂章有人搭起了白色的舞台
以笨重的身軀疊起團結的圖案
但今夜你穿了疲倦的黑衣
臉上遺失了歡愉的表情是因為
不習慣璀璨的氣氛還是
太慣於靜默的表達？

and suddenly I couldn't be certain
of the true outlines
of this city and you

Imagine this city were already old
how long could we stay young?

After midnight passed
it was said another era was beginning
broken beer bottles dotted the road
and the shattered glass flashed with dark green light
we paused and looked around
for the way we'd come
the insubstantial wind stirred our restless hair
I kept close to you
listening to a drunkard's song disperse across the dark deserted alley
cheers came from the other end of the street
how should we find our way into this new century?

The journey to the century
began with a New Year's festival
bright red, brilliant and jubilant
people in ethnic dress danced
with a sleepy golden dragon while others sawed out squeaky tunes
on the *huqin* and others put up a white stage
and piled a symbol of unity on its heavy body
but that night you wore tired black clothing
had your face lost its happy expression because
you're not used to rowdiness or
you're too used to silence?

聚滿人群的廣場我們走過
一座新近矗立水中的亭園
朱紅的飛簷勾起了歷史與文化
抽象的括弧
立法局大樓洶湧傳來
米高風擴大了的論辯
離開圍觀的鎂光燈我們繞著大樓
走了一個圈子
不是為了悼念即將隱沒的圓柱與拱廊
祇是微雨的昏夜我們無從躲閃
翳悶混濁的空氣
我們仰視樓頂女神手持的天秤
侷促地呼吸下一個世紀的夜空
閃電藏於天的右邊
燈火與歌聲盛放於左邊
企立在曖昧的中央地帶
我祇想抓緊一個實在的身影
你低頭看我
我轉頭去看八面玲瓏的燈飾
相反相成的人潮裏
我倆單薄如落在地上的雨花

雨花越織越大
道路與睡意漸漸傾斜
側著肩膊看你濃密的眉毛
問你能否讓我知道：
當我們開始蒼老
這個城市還可以年輕多久？

We walked past a public square full of people
and a pavilion newly erected on the water
the flying vermillion evoked the abstract brackets
of history and culture
an amplified debate
blared out of the Legislative Council Building
we left the camera lights
and circled the building
not grieving the columns and arches that were about to vanish
we just couldn't avoid the light rain
and heavy wet air
we looked up to the roof where the goddess held her heavenly scales
and uneasily breathed in a new century's night air
lightning burrowed into the right side of the sky
lights and singing filled the left side
standing on tiptoe in the uncertain middle ground
I wanted to hold on tight to something real
you looked down at me
I turned to watch the colorful lights
in the streams of people
we were breakable as the raindrops hitting the ground

The rain started to fall harder
the street inclined and so did our drowsiness
Leaning my shoulder toward your thick eyebrows
I asked you:
when we start to get old
how long can this city stay young?

詩錄旺角

走進日劇的光碟市場走進
戀愛世代的悠長假期
身體與身體擠壓的空間沒有
走火防火的通道上來來回回
尋找被時間遺棄於路旁
一個掉在過去的笑容
轉角有羞赧的琴聲滑動
猶豫的指頭青春原來是
獨自坐在虛空的房子內的意志
Would you still hang around
佈滿傢俱的空鏡凝聚鏡內鏡外
等待的焦慮
我挪前一步避去人群站在後面的急躁
差點便給擠進了電視的熒幕裏
當主角的眼睛湊近我的臉龐時
竟瞥見你我的類像　刹那
瀟灑滿地驚疑的喜怒哀樂
再給前呼後擁的鞋印踩成
不合規格的翻版光碟

A Poem of Mong Kok

1. Sino Center (*take two*)

Into the daily drama of the CD store and into
a long holiday after a time of love
there's no space between the body and the pressure of bodies
walking up and down the fire lanes
looking for a roadside abandoned by time
a smile left in the past
at the corner the sound of bashful strings sliding
a springtime of hesitant fingers once
sat alone in an empty room of determination
Would you still hang around
the camera shot of furniture coalesces the anxiety of waiting
on either side of the lens
I step away from the impatience of the people behind me
nearly squeezing myself into the TV screen
when the lead's eyes lean close to my face
they almost catch a glance of us   in an instant
an explosion of bewildering human emotion floods in
and the footprints of the crowd are pressed into
unauthorized CDs

2. 先達廣場 (take one)

像啟動的攝影機
你以光的速度游行於
一堆身體互相擠壓推撞的空隙之間
金田一、怪醫秦博士還有
永遠孩子氣的木村拓哉與常常
喜歡聳肩的松隆子
你願意把誰的笑容攝入
自己的臉上
追隨你的光速像吉田超人飛行的姿勢我害怕
終會變成宇宙的黑點因為
逃生的前門已被熒光屏的激光堵住
我們的關係便必須
因為後無退路而義無反顧
但當連續劇結束的時候你還沒有
告訴我有沒有續集的可能?

2. Sin Tat Plaza (*take one*)

Like switching on a camera
you march at the speed of light
through the gaps between bodies that bump and press together,
the Kindaichi Case Files and Dr. Black Jack manga,
the eternally childlike singer Kimura Takuya
and Takako Matsu who likes to shrug her shoulders
you want to project someone else's smile
onto your own face
following you at Ultraman speed I fear
you'll become a stain on the universe because
the escape door is blocked by the screen's laser beams
and our relationship can't
turn back since there's nowhere to retreat to
but when the TV series finishes will you still not
have told me if there's the possibility of a sequel?

3. 信和中心 (flash back)

佈滿廢紙的自動電梯上下移動
像穿過兩條方向相反的時光隧道
我從戀愛世代的悠長假期中回來
帶著回憶的膠卷在倒轉的空間裏
尋找人物與情節兌現的可能
you're on my mind
反光的玻璃柱上我看見身後
兩個不同的熒光屏放著相同的畫面
遊戲節目的主持人賣力地演出
各種滑稽的動作例如把手掌掉到
鍋裏煮湯再用驚呼的表情
把圓形的嘴巴拉成
三角的圖案然後吻在鏡頭上
我緊緊盯著銀幕上跳動的肢體卻沒有
發笑的衝動　　祇有
台北高速滑動的虹影在心跳的軸輪上
漸漸凝住一張臉孔的黑白
離開這城市一段日子
日劇的熱賣已改變了內容
光影的世代裏我們往往祇能抓住
一些匆匆的顏色和聲音
祇有記憶和想像才是現世的
爬過城市的邊緣
甩掉歷史的承諾
我們才不會擦身而過

3. Sino Center (*flash back*)

Escalators littered with trash run up and down
like two tunnels traveling with and against time
I've come back from a long holiday from love
carrying a filmroll of memory that turns backward in space
searching for the possibility of character and plot resolution
you're on my mind
in a reflection in the glass I see what's behind me
two different screens showing the same show
the host spares no effort in his performance
with lots of amusing movements like dropping his hands
into boiling soup and then letting his alarmed expression
elongate his round mouth
into a triangular shape that kisses the camera
I stare at the body jumping about on the screen but
have no impulse to laugh   there's only
Taipei's rainbowed image gliding on a heartbeat's axle
gradually solidifying into a black and white face
leaving this city for a while
the daily drama of hot sales have changed their content
in this time of light and shadow we often can only grasp
a few fleeting colors and sounds
without memory and imagination it wouldn't be this life
only when we pass the city limits
only when we throw off history's commitments
will we be more than just passing through

老媽和黑貓

聽說黑貓
最具有不為人知的異能

自從你闖入家門後
媽的皺紋因笑容而增多了
抹著你通體烏亮的毛髮
側耳諦聽你牙牙學語
或拿著毛巾追在你的腿後
媽回到初為人母的時候

早上的陽光總要在驟雨過後
才透進屋子來
又濕又熱的窗台外
聽不懂媽跟你嘰呢呱啦些甚麼
隔著玻璃的門縫看見你
懶懶的拉長了軟綿綿的身軀
也拉長媽單薄的時間
綠色的眼睛會不會也看出一個青蔥的世界
讓陽光和驟雨永遠明麗?
媽的手在你背上來回撫摸
和著彼此低沉的呼吸有如微風的節奏
再有一陣雨灑過
一點陽光飄落
我聽見你清脆的喵了一聲

My Mom and the Black Cat

I've heard that black cats
possess the strangest talents unknown to man

Ever since you snuck into her house
my mom has more laugh-lines
brushing your glossy black fur
listening attentively to you prattle
or taking a towel to your legs
she can return to her first days of being a mother

The morning sunshine waits until the rainstorms have passed
to flood into the room
the hot humidity outside
can't understand what my mom chirps at you
between the glass door and its frame I see you
sluggishly stretching out your plush body
stretching out my mom's thinning time
can green eyes still perceive a green world
keeping the sunlight and sudden rain bright forever?
Mom's hand strokes your back
and you soften each other's breathing to the rhythm of a breeze
another rain shower sprinkles past
a hint of sunshine floats down
I hear your single clear *meow*

媽說你喜歡吃雞肉和排骨
眷戀人的膝蓋　常常吻她的臉頰
又說你喜歡追逐紙團和繩索
而且把地氈和藤鞭都變成玩具
每個晚上踏入家門
媽的話題改變了
不再討論粵語殘片的好看與難堪
不再打電話找已經離家的兒子
不再抱著發黃的照片努力辨認自己
卻絮絮不休今天你吃了多少
打碎了幾隻杯子
咬破了幾件傢具
聽說家貓能活十五年的生命
算計那個時候
媽會在天堂活得年輕
而我卻要為了你的離去
把額上的歲月拉成貓紋
瞧著這一間空屋一個老媽和一隻小貓
心中默禱可以和你們莫失莫忘

Mom says you like to eat chicken and spareribs
you love knees   and you often kiss her cheeks
she says you like to chase crumpled paper and cords
and you turn the rug and rattan into toys
each night when you come inside
my mom changes the subject
no longer does she discuss good and bad Cantonese films
no longer does she call her son who's left home
no longer does she hold up yellowing photos to pick herself out
she just goes on and on about how much you ate today
broke how many glasses
chewed on how many pieces of furniture
I've heard that a housecat can live for fifteen years
and I figure that when that happens
my mom will still be young in heaven
and because of your leaving
the years will spread in leopard-print across my forehead
look: in this empty room, my mom and a small cat
I silently pray I won't lose either of you

自我紙盒藏屍的日子

患病的身體捲曲、怕光
畏懼聲音　然而喜歡潮濕
這是一段自我紙盒藏屍的日子
我用收縮的瞳孔
擴張四面紙壁的闊度
看見自己腐化的心逐漸變硬
而且晶瑩透亮

在熬過二百四十四天後
我從紙盒爬出　在嚴寒的低溫搭上
有空調的長途巴士　（如同另一個鐵盒）
從光天白日走到烏天黑地
這城市有人、有燈
車子走在半空　從天橋望入樓房
晃動的人影　電視藍色的聲浪
悠揚播送飯香
轉入直路車輪差點碰撞行人的腳跟
紅紅綠綠的減價招牌
跟熒光屏上的廣告歌曲互相吆喝
我想　聖誕節也快來臨了
然後是新年　元宵　情人節
清明和復活節　週而復始
怎麼辦呢這麼連綿無盡的節日氣氛？

走得累了是這一雙滿佈紅絲的眼睛
有閃光的暈眩　無法分辨
城市密集的燈影和人群

Days When I Hide My Corpse in a Cardboard Box

This sick body curls up, fears the light
dreads sound   but likes the damp
these are the days I hide my corpse in a cardboard box
I see through contracted pupils
my rotting heart hardening bit by bit
turning glittering and transparent

After enduring two hundred forty-four days
I climb out of the box   and in the hypothermic cold
take a heated long distance bus (another steel box)
from the bright daylight to the black night
in the city there are people and streetlamps,
cars drive through midair   I can see into buildings from the overpass
the swaying shadows of people   blue clamor of televisions
the far-wafting scent of cooking
turning, the bus wheels almost hit the pedestrians' heels
red and green sales signs
and fluorescent advertising jingles shout at each other
I think   Christmas must be coming
and then it's New Years   Lantern Festival   Valentine's Day
Grave-Sweeping Day and Easter   year after year after year
how do we deal with these continuous interminable holidays?

What's tired now are these bloodshot eyes
dizzy from the flashes   unable to distinguish
the city's dense lights and groups of people

幸福的節日祝禱馬上就要開始
怎麼辦呢這麼繁盛的喧囂？
父母帶著孩子上車下車
情侶挽著手臂從車頭走到車尾
祇有老人走得最慢最不被原諒
怎麼辦呢這麼容易被擠跌的空間？

終於車子也駛過你當日
從高空躍下的酒店門口
撞毀的鐵欄已經修補　血跡和鮮花
都已成新聞圖片　這城市
總有新的燈飾替換每日的故事
從車窗隔著玻璃望向逐漸收窄的港灣
我們有理由相信　明年今日
是必須延續下去的！

在不能忍受新陳代謝與新舊交替的情況下
最後我還是決定再過一段
自我紙盒藏屍的日子
戒掉水、希望和光
好好跟自己相處

the holiday well-wishing is about to begin
how do we deal with all the commotion?
Parents take their children on and off the bus
lovers go arm in arm from the front of the bus to the back
the slow-moving elderly are least likely to be forgiven
how do we deal with such a packed jostling space?

Finally the bus drives passes the entrance
of the hotel from whose heights you leapt that day
the shattered steel fence has been repaired   the blood stains and flowers
are just pictures in the news   in this city
there are always new neon lights switching stories every day
looking out through the window at the gradually narrowing harbor
we have reason to believe   that next year
will still go on!

I can't stand all this change from old to new
so in the end I decide to spend more time
hiding my corpse in a cardboard box
I give up water, hope, and light
and get along quite well with myself

與我名字相關的顏色

那一天我在行人道上聽著雷射音樂的時候
卻突然站下來遠遠的看見了你
穿著一件紅色上衣
截停一輛紅色的計程車
於是我便慌忙地撐起一把藍色的雨傘
遮住蒼白的天空
因為天空正下著細雨……

耳筒的音樂從飛機降落地面
不穩定的氣流輕微的震音支配我的心跳和呼吸
再度回到這個城市
維多利亞港變成了狹窄的小河
青翠的花園越建越多
新的購物廣場有了時代的名字
大抵我的髮型和思想都該改換程式吧
這個夏季
仍然流行去年雪紡造的長裙
透明的布料重重疊疊造成不透明的
你的表情

電影的顏色是苦澀的歌曲的旋律是
鬱藍的但我並沒有
那麼恆久傷感的力量
所以將來某一天
假如我又在一條不相干的行人道上遇見你
請不要穿那同樣的衣裳
　　截停同樣的計程車
因為那是與我名字相關的顏色
這樣會使我繼續疑惑
直到白頭

The Color of My Name

That day I was listening to music on the sidewalk
I stopped short and caught sight of you in the distance
wearing a red jacket
stopping a red cab
I opened a blue umbrella
to block out the gray sky
as it started to drizzle . . .

The music in my earphones lands with the plane
the tremolo of turbulence sets my heartbeat and breath
returning once more to this city
Victoria Harbor has narrowed to a stream
more green gardens are being built
new shopping centers are named for the times
my hairstyle and way of thinking should probably change
this summer
last year's chiffon dresses are still in vogue
the transparent fabric layered into opacity
like your expression

Movies' colors are bitter songs' melodies are
blue but I don't have
the strength for such persistent sadness
so supposing some day in the future
on some irrelevant sidewalk I catch sight of you
please don't be wearing the same clothes
stopping the same cab
because that's the color of my name
and it would cause me to doubt
until my hair turned white

八號風波

趕在八號風球的季節裏
用一個無從轉身的姿勢
登上高飛的七四七客機
把悲傷留給自己
而亂雲托起的心思
就留給風雨飄搖的城市

趕不及在風平浪靜的日子
向你道歉和道別
白雲藍天的歲月
如今已遠遠給拋在背後
當客機在雷電中隆隆昇起的刹那
我便已認命
知道無法抓住時間的尾巴

趕在仍然年輕的時候
可以默然地坦然地
坐在深水的港灣
觀看眼前一幕一幕記憶的風暴
雨從時間的針尖刺落
兩岸的燈火璀璨如血

趕不及在你仍然美麗的時刻
在你面前展現一個如你一般美麗的我
香港的秋天總是令人心平氣和的
曠遠的藍天磊落光明
你的笑容清新而不腐朽

Tropical Storm No. 8

In the season of typhoon warnings
with no way to turn back
I boarded a 747
keeping sadness for myself
keeping the thoughts evoked by the chaotic clouds
for the city buffeted by wind and rain

There wasn't time on those tranquil days
to apologize and say goodbye
the time of white clouds and blue sky
has long since been abandoned
when the plane climbs into the rumbling thunder and lightning
I accept my fate
knowing I can't grab onto time's tail

There is still time to be young
to silently and calmly
sit by the deep harbor
and watch storm after storm play out from memory
rain falls from the needlepricks of time
lights on the two banks shine bright as blood

When you were beautiful there wasn't time
to unfold before you my equally beautiful self
autumn in Hong Kong always cheers people up
the sky is open and bright
your smile is pure not decadent

祇是
既誕生於風雨的夏季
我便必需在秋天來臨之前離去

仍然趕得及嗎?
餘下的數百個日子
足夠讓你忘記讓我緊記
歷史?
歷史是不會轉身迎向秋天的
當我再度回來的時候
你的心事
仍會不會刮起八級風暴呢?

it's just that
born in the summer rains
I must leave before autumn arrives

Is there still time?
Are these remaining few hundred days enough
to make you forget and make me remember
history?
History will not turn back to meet autumn
and when I return
will your secrets
still be whipping up gale-force winds?

十月城岸的病忘書

當暈眩的身體淌成了旋轉的石頭
城市的排水道有煙火爆裂的聲音
凹陷的河床裏我是飄離的蜉蝣
游動死光的白與青草的腐壞
撕裂一張人臉　再一張自己的臉
裂縫的眼神載滿了沙泥
便揉不進一句訣別的話
病毒在脈搏的支流跳舞
從狐步的腹瀉到探戈的感冒
再轉入霹靂的咳嗽
混濁的呼吸和水流並沒有因為覺悟的高燒
重新開啟宿命的港灣
你依舊攜著激石的尖削走過光滑的堤岸
一步一步割斷風聲的衣帶
諾言帶著它的玻璃碎片
去堆砌從此快快樂樂的虹橋
橋上的青春裝飾著缺月的窗
橋下的死亡熱烈地唱和無字詞的歌
我和你從未如此遙遙的接近
在水聲吞吐或嘔吐的遲疑間
歲月在抽搐
抽成你曾經許願的那張白頁
我用沾墨的水草狠力的抹過
便抹成你我蒼老的顏色
於是　最後　你也不能倖免

October in the City: A Book of Amnesia

When dizzied bodies drip into spinning stones
the city's drains ring with the boom of firecrackers
and I'm a fluttering mayfly in the sunken riverbed
disturbing the whiteness of the dead light and the putrefying grass
tearing at someone's face   then tearing my own face
riven gaze filled with mud
and a word of farewell can't be rubbed in
viruses dance through the pulse of the tributaries
from foxtrot diarrhea to tango flu
becoming thunderous coughing
turbid breath and rivers haven't reopened the harbor of fate
with fevered enlightenment
you still carry pointed rocks over the smooth embankments
step by step cutting the sash of rumors
promises carry glass splinters
to pile up on the newly-happy arched bridge
on the bridge youth decorates a moonless window
below the bridge death belts out a lyric-less song
you and I have never approached from so far before
in the hesitation of the water's vomits or stammers
time twitches
and turns into that white page you once wished upon
I've ruthlessly smeared it with the ink of water weeds
smeared it into the color of our old age
and so   in the end   you can't escape

當病患的城市躺成佔領的石頭
身體的暗渠響動了甦醒的意識
未明的天空有團結的雲塊
推著地面的人潮揚起了布幔和標語
有人有燈的角落便有色光的奔流
霓虹的手影牽著環抱的線圈
從上游的心臟地帶流轉中游的肺腑邊緣
再匯合下游的群情洶湧
撐起雨傘的街道像斑爛的蘑菇堡壘
護著城門的河　河上被磨蝕的土層
黑色的暴雷或暴徒從四方八面鞭起了火舌
佔領的人群退潮後又滔滔的復返
你企圖越過封鎖的防線向我走來
但抖顫的手腳使你縮成光源狹小的街燈
單薄地釘在情感安全的河套
當時局的潮汐向前滾動你便身不由己的後退
退成模糊零落的焦距
逐漸消失於煙霧喧鬧的黃昏
然後城牆倒塌　你爬到內河的危岸
帶著禿髮的頭　多骨節的手
再度誕生的我　早已記認不得你了

當自由的河道不再淤塞
活存的流域可以選擇自己的出口
廢墟的城市開滿了青草與黃花
天亮時份　我便與你從此不再相見

When the sick city lies down and becomes an occupied stone
the canals of the body stir the consciousness awake
the unlit sky draws clumps of clouds
pushing the people below toward raised banners and posters
some people find lit corners where colored light pours out
neon shadow puppets hold the encircled coils
heartfelt fringes flow from the heartland's upper reaches to the midlands
and converge with the turbulent public courage of the lower reaches
the streets of umbrellas are like multicolored mushroom fortresses
guarding the city's moats   the moats' layers of eroded soil
dark thunder or mobs whip up flames in all directions
the occupiers ebb away and then surge back in
you try to cross the defensive blockades toward me
but with your trembling hands and feet you shrink into a street lamp
feebly pinned to the river bend of secure emotion
when the tides of the times toss you backward
and you become an indistinct point in the distance
with the smoky noisy dawn disappearing bit by bit
and the city walls collapse   you crawl to the dangerous shores
                    of an interior river
with your bald head   and many-jointed hands
and the reborn me   can't recognize you anymore

When the time comes that the river of freedom doesn't silt up
the flow of deposits can choose its own exit
and the ruins of the city will bloom with plants and chrysanthemums
when daylight comes   you and I will never meet again

現代豪俠傳

祇有忽然倦透的
是我的一雙手
倦於說話和比劃
倦於做飯、洗衣和寫信
倦於遊蕩
倦於疲倦
所以我便有四個藉口三個理由
頹廢地坐在熒光幕前
讓它休息
讓它沉默
而不溫柔

　　電影裏有這樣的鏡頭：
　　當了母親的女飛俠抱著自己的女娃娃
　　黑色的房間內盪來盪去
　　然後又攜著聖誕火雞
　　來到灰色的戰場尋找丈夫
　　卻換來丈夫暴烈的責罵
　　因為戰場不是女人的歸宿
　　這時
　　顛倒錯亂的人群失常地四散奔逃
　　白色的煙塵裏凝固了女飛俠一張憔悴的臉
　　偶然一個回眸的近鏡
　　妻子、母親和飛俠的角色便驟然失去了焦距
　　額前一綹髮絲疲傭地垂下
　　音樂在喧嘩的槍聲中響起──

Tale of a Modern Day Knight

What's suddenly utterly exhausted
is my hands
tired of talking and gesturing
tired of cooking and doing laundry and writing letters
tired of waving
tired of being tired
so I have four excuses and three reasons
to sit here decadently in front of the fluorescent screen
to let them rest
to let them be silent
rather than gentle and soft

       Here are some scenes from the movie:
       the heroine holds her baby daughter
       she sways inside a dark room
       then carrying a holiday turkey
       she goes to the gray battlefield to look for her husband
       but she is scolded fiercely by him
       because a battlefield is no place for a woman
       at that moment
       the chaotic crowd scatters
       and in the white smoke of war the heroine's thin face solidifies
       the camera zooms in
       and the roles of wife, mother and heroine suddenly lose focus
       a lock of hair falls wearily over her forehead
       music rings out over the clamor of gunshots——

慶幸我們都各自找到彼此
疲倦和失望的理由
而無須這樣驚天動地驚心動魄
慶幸我們的瑣碎與平凡
比電影的剪接出色比襯景的音效
更充滿技巧
譬如說
你愛把寶藍的襯衣配上米色的西褲
再架上隱形眼鏡隱去現實的不協調
例如我喜歡把長髮編成不合比例的辮子
把怨言與想望故意甩成身後揚散的紙屑
我們企立於熱鬧的人群之中
用滿不在乎的微笑消磨四方八面的言語
直到有一天
電影和音樂都聲嘶力竭了
我們才回到蒼白頹敗的佈景裏——

    蒼白頹敗的佈景裏此刻
    男主角倒臥人群凌亂的腳下
    槍聲與歌聲響得更急
    女主角失神的衣角
    給鐵欄割成碎片
    男主角舉起受傷的右手
    似是求援又似是責備
    在人為的亂世與人造的畫面割切下
    跪在丈夫身前的女人便再也站不起來了

慶幸我們的故事比電影更直接了當
就如你曾經為我安排這最後的一幕：
委派A和B擔當慰問的角色
卻吩咐C以更漂亮動人的風采站在你的身旁

Fortunately we find each other
reasons to be exhausted and disappointed
and there's no need for such drama
fortunately our ordinariness
is more extraordinary than snippets of film, more skillful
than a scene's sound effects
for example
you like to pair bright blue shirts with cream-colored pants
and then put in contact lenses to hide anything that doesn't match
for example I like to put my hair up into a disproportionately thick braid
and scatter complaints and desires behind me like scraps of paper
we stand on tiptoe in the midst of a lively crowd
wearing down the talk on all sides with nonchalant smiles
and only when
the movies and music wear themselves out
will we return to the faded overdone movie set——

    at this moment on the faded overdone movie set
    the hero lies beneath the crowd's crazed feet
    the gunfire and music have grown more urgent
    the heroine's poor clothing
    has been shredded by a fence
    the hero lifts his injured right hand
    as though to beg for help or as if in blame
    cut off by that chaotic manmade world and synthetic tableau
    the woman kneeling at her husband's side won't get up again

Fortunately our stories are more straightforward than the movies
consider how you arranged this final scene for me:
give A and B the role of offering condolences
but tell the more beautiful and elegant C to stand beside you

無須生離死別你期望
驚險的情節賦予你任重道遠的形象
而我竟也沒有使你的期望落空
慢慢走出注視的人群早已圈劃的視框
卻沒有讓鏡頭在你的隱形鏡片上印下
任何猶豫或深情的臉容
因為我也慣於搬演
讓你永遠後悔和懷念的決絕

都疲倦了吧
那麼就關掉電影
讓彼此的手
停在風中安睡吧
停成永不道破的符號
那或許是一個圓圈、一個圖案、一個字母
甚至一個謎語、一句詩
但我知道那絕對不是一個
盟誓

no need to abandon your dreams
the plot will symbolically shoulder them for you
and I have never stood in the way
I'll slowly walk away from the crowd's demarcated gaze
but your contact lenses won't capture
any hint of hesitation or love in the scene
because I'm used to reenacting
this separation that you always endlessly regret

We're both tired
let's turn off the movie
and let each other's hands
sleep soundly in the breeze
stop in the form of an ambiguous symbol
perhaps it's a circle, a pattern, a letter
even a riddle, a line of poetry
but I know it absolutely isn't
a vow

Biographies

Natalia S. H. CHAN (Pseudonym: Lok Fung) is a poet and cultural critic. She received her PhD in Comparative Literature & Cultural Studies from The University of California, San Diego, and is currently an Adjunct Assistant Professor in the Department of Cultural & Religious Studies at the Chinese University of Hong Kong. Her research interests include film and cultural theory, gender studies, popular culture, performance studies, comparative literature, cross-dressing and fashion.

Her creative works include three volumes of poetry entitled *Distance*, *Dislocation*, and *Flying Coffin*, as well as two volumes of short stories entitled *The Last Fairy Tale* and *The Carbon-Burning City*. Her critical works include *Butterfly of Forbidden Colors: The Artistic Image of Leslie Cheung*, *Please Stand Behind the Yellow Line: Traces of Time in Hong Kong Literature*, *Lyrical Writing of Light and Shadow*, *Dancing in the Maze* and *Gender-Crossing: Male Impersonation in Hong Kong Cinema*.

Eleanor Goodman is a Research Associate at the Harvard University Fairbank Center, and spent a year at Peking University on a Fulbright Fellowship. She has been an artist in residence at the American Academy in Rome and was awarded a Henry Luce Translation Fellowship from the Vermont Studio Center. Her first book of translations, *Something Crosses My Mind: Selected Poems of Wang Xiaoni* (Zephyr Press, 2014) was the recipient of a 2013 PEN/Heim Translation Grant and winner of the 2015 Lucien Stryk Prize. The book was also shortlisted for the International Griffin Prize. Her anthology *Iron Moon*, a translation of Chinese worker's poetry (White Pine Press), was released in the spring of 2017, and her translation of *The Roots of Wisdom: Poems by Zang Di* was released in the fall of 2017